WINNER OF THE

DE NOVO POETRY PRIZE

2013

RIVER BOUND

River Bound

BRIAN SIMONEAU

C&R PRESS

PRESS

FIRST EDITION PAPERBACK

ISBN-13: 978-1-936196-36-4
ISBN-10: 1-936196-36-0
LCCN: 2013958052

Foggy Morning in Manotick
Photography © 2014 by
Danielle Donders

Book interior & cover design
by Terrence Chouinard
The typeface is
Fournier.

In memory of Arthur O. Simoneau

1946–2004

for Amelia & Harper

ONE

Mill Town: Variations · *3*

Nor'easter · *7*

After a Student Prefaces Her

Question about a Poem · *9*

Morning Mass · *10*

Poem for My Brother · *11*

Lowell National Historic Park · *12*

The Canal · *14*

City Champs Celebrate Unlikely

Win in Back of Coach's Pickup · *15*

Season's End · *17*

Taking Flight · *19*

Appleton & Pearl · *20*

Dust · *22*

To the Guy Who Stole My Bike · *24*

Each Pleasure · *25*

My Father's Garage as Resting Place · *28*

The Truth Is · *30*

TWO

Because This Life Is Brief · *35*

Shopping for Pants as Lesson in Language · *36*

The Memory Endeavors to Bear Its Own Weight · *37*

Funeral with Cherry Blossoms Falling · *39*

Sonnet for the Guy Who Told Me

My Dad Was a Saint · *42*

Elegy with a Chance of Rain · *43*

[untitled] · *45*

November: Almost New Moon · 46

Song · 47

New Year's Eve · 48

Poem with the Glimmer of Ice in a Tree · 49

Late March · 51

As If Souls Really Do Ascend · 52

The Gravedigger to the Grieving Poet · 54

Spring Comes to Lowell · 55

Portrait of My Father as a Mountain · 57

Lines from Wherever My Father Finds Himself · 58

THREE

North of Stinson Beach · 63

Tending the Fire · 64

Ceiling: Unlimited · 65

Prayer · 66

Tonight I Walked in the Shadow of a Tree · 68

Even a Beach in Winter · 69

After Rain · 70

Working the Garden · 72

Poem with Snowy Plovers · 74

Under a Summer Sky · 75

At a Horseshoe Bend in the Rogue · 76

A Constant Reminder · 77

Life After Life · 79

Where I Come From the Snow's Beginning To Stick · 81

Like a Chance to Begin Again · 82

Something of Home · 83

ACKNOWLEDGEMENTS · 87

You left and couldn't leave that dirty river town
where every day the dirty river rolls.

RICHARD HUGO
Last Words to James Wright

ONE

Mill Town: Variations

A desert of commerce, flash floods
of financial focus (textiles,
computers, commuter condos)
forever receding, washed out
devastated homes, cobblestones
crumbled, miles of boarded-up glass,
mirror-windowed high rise empty,
no one to take in its vistas:
the mills grainy cold in shadow
despite the sunlight stretched along
each length of smokestack, cracks opened
where mortar begins, has begun,
began when the first stone was laid
to come apart, collapsing mote
by falling mote into redbrick
canyons, canals carving channels
to the river, Boston, beyond.

A roadside attraction, wayside
makeshift memorial, commons
growing gardens where factory
carcasses crumbled, new museums
around the brick and rafter bones
of boardinghouses, markets, mills,
monuments made from waterwheels,
a national park, concert hall,
baseball stadium, all of it
advertised on highways that skirt
this place like streams working their way
past storm-wreck: urban renewal,
decay reclaimed, oasis of
smokestack and brick, bridges spanning
windowed canyons and the river
sliding along, its constant rise
and fall, a future in its wake.

3

A working ghost town, endless rows
of dim windows, cemetery
of factory stacks reflected
in quiet canals, Merrimack
making its constant exodus
to sea, names engraved in granite
lintels (Appleton, Boott, Lawrence,
Wannalancit) no longer signs
of progress, promises of work
for all, families and immigrants
and girls who abandoned themselves
to the boardinghouse from the farm,
each street sign telling forgotten
tales (Pawtucket, Market, Moody,
Dutton), stretches of cobblestone
coming apart: each tattered thread
a phantom on a fading map.

4

A marketplace constellation,
pattern of pinpricks stitched along
riverbanks, clusters of redbrick
mills revisioned as malls, condos,
companies coming like comets,
every revolution brighter
than before, the flash and fizzle
amounting to nothing but more
of the same: darkness, vacant space
and darkness, history tracing
its path, the past spinning into
place, edges frayed, every city
consuming itself, collapsing
under the weight—a galaxy
given over to gravity's
pull, all of it gathered around
an inevitable black hole.

Nor'easter

It's no wonder
    people leave. Thirty inches
in less than a day, more
    on its way. No wonder

few come back: grown men
    scolded for tracking mud
in the house, slush
    and gutter-muck. Even if

it's pure, untouched
    by trucks and stomping boots,
everyone knows it'll stop
    and the weather warm to show

the same gray streets
    and spring a long way off—
winter in Lowell,
    hardly a hill to sled.

A plow rumbles down
    the block, wipes out an hour
of hard labor. Still
    a blade of yellow grass

works its way
      through slush beneath my feet
and a broken back
      can't get more broke. I listen:

after the echo
      of shovel scraping sidewalk,
my heartbeat.
      My breath rises up.

I'm clearing
      a path so I can
get out, a trail
      I can follow back in.

After a Student Prefaces Her Question about a Poem

I want to stop her, tell her I don't know much
about poetry either. I know about scrubbing toilets,
pumping gas and fixing cars, tearing apart
old fences and the rotting walls of sheds,
painting someone else's house. I've heard
the rhythms of engines breaking down,
wrenches dropped on concrete floors.

I taught myself to sing in filth, foot tapping in time
with ticking generators, dripping faucets, cooling
engines, pounding hammers. Trucks, garages,
basement workshops resounding with my voice:
ammonia, bleach, denatured alcohol, poly-
urethane, oil-based, latex paint, rubber gloves,
sawdust, rusty water running down cinder blocks.

I learned not to hold my breath for answers. Listen,
every poem poses a chance like this: we work our way
through its rooms—rubbing surfaces raw, stripping
walls to studs, putting them splinter by splinter back
till we're stuck with a pile of leftover parts—
and we raise a hand for help, asking to be
numbered among the great unwashed.

Morning Mass

Sunday sunlight washes over families holding hands
like paper dolls. Before breaking bread, heads bend
to pray: eyes closed, lips moving in union with the priest's

whose arms unfold as if to grasp the holy air.
Candles lift whispers of smoke toward heavens
that hover somewhere above a vaulted ceiling.

Faith forgotten by Monday morning: heads
again hang low; hard voices mutter
curses against brothers, bosses, the blind sun

scorching the sky; empty hands reach out to find
what's left to grasp. Every day they handle hammers
and wrenches, shovels, brushes, brooms. Every day

consumes them, flames of foundries and factories
and their own hands stoke the furnace, the sweat
sharp on blistered skin. Every day wears down

their bodies—crumpled pages, torn to pieces,
tossed by a wind that muffles prayers and pleas
and cries for love or something like it, mercy.

Poem for My Brother

We're not white trash, my brother said
to the kid who'd taken his hat.
He told my brother to shut up;
then he punched him in the stomach.
The early morning stung my eyes,
a church bell sounded in my head,
my lips quivered, let out a breath.
And I punched his ugly face once
then twice then over and over
until my knuckles burned and I
couldn't tell if the blood was his
or mine. He cried for me to stop.
My brother cried as well but
softly and without a word. Years
later, he tells me that he cried
because it seemed I never would.
My eyes were someplace else. Empty,
he says, or filled with something he'd
never seen until that morning.
He cried, he tells me, for brothers
unable to speak under cracked
open skies, morning light flooding
their mouths like blood, lips pressed against
prayer as they watch each other break.

Lowell National Historic Park

Cherry trees along the canal struggle
    out of winter. Red brick ripples
on the surface, laps against rotting

    leaves, beer cans, graffiti. From the bridge
beside the old church, you can hear it coming:
    drone, babble of motorboat, chattering tour.

Middlesex Canal, twenty-eight miles to Boston;
    forty mills by 1850, hundreds
of water-wheels, thousands of looms spinning;

    foreign dignitaries came to see this
country at its finest; unions, strikers,
    riots, Industrial Workers of the World.

No one's listening, and even if
    they heard *Wobblies* they'd likely assume
it's a local bird. They're told about mill girls

    but there's no mention of how many threw
themselves, nameless, down to the water.
    Some one notices the architecture

of the windows. No one sees the empty
    storefront displays, most of downtown
out of business and not on the tour. No one

asks about the shopping carts huddled beneath
the bridge, about workers who kept coming
      long after the trickle of work went dry.

If you're not from here, it's hard to see
      that every year the waters rise and fall
and cherry trees struggle through the longest

      winters. If you are, you watch each blossom
tumble to the water's edge and settle in grass
      that sways, unbroken, in the passing wake.

The Canal

A shopping cart lies on its side, its empty plastic trash bags pasted with mud like tattered sails clinging to a wreck. Half-buried bottles and cans are treasures for someone to dig up—kids who swim here, splashing and laughing even after tales of rats as big as dogs and ghosts of mill girls drowned in black water. A truck tire hangs from a branch. One of them tosses his cap aside and climbs high: long swing over water before the sudden drop, splash, plunge—all the way down where who knows what he'll find. When the sun gives up behind smokestacks, they run from the scrape of a cane on gravel and glass. One of them stays behind, replaces the cap on his head, and takes a step toward the man weaving back to his cart. They look at each other and glimpse what hides inside. One hurries home with a ghost in tow. One settles in mud and leans against the trunk to drink what nickels bought today. He watches the moonrise, its reflection broken by his shadow swaying as he pisses in the canal and curses the sound of a crying child somewhere in the dark.

City Champs Celebrate Unlikely Win in Back of Coach's Pickup

They look almost like men: dusty, stripped
to T-shirts, caps backwards, cheeks packed
with sunflower seeds and Big League Chew
like it's Red Man, chanting, hooting at girls
on the corner, old folks on a porch, dark
windows of school. Dogs bark back, a star
looks down and they hold their breath
past the cemetery—it's bad luck not to,
and walk-off or not, no one wants to push it
and miss the banana splits and beautiful babes
at the counter by dropping dead right now
because tonight might be like nothing
they've ever known before, so you better
believe they'll hold their breath. By the time
Coach slows into the Frosty Boy lot,
benchwarmers wave spotless shirts like banners,
fists pumping muggy air, and the one who hit
the winning shot—long fly that finally dropped
with slow-motion-movie thud against the hill—
holds court on a wheel well, hands
working the ball, turning it over and over,
tracing every stitch, every stitch
an idea of leaving none of them
would ever speak out loud, getting out
of here the goal that goes for them all

but goes unsaid. Instead they're singing
Queen and keeping an eye on his hands
around the ball. JB, Gene-O Reno, Scooter,
Skip. They know what's what: he won
and they're along for the ride; they'll have
to step aside when he takes off and maybe
never makes it back or—what they fear most
but don't know it yet—makes his way home
when he can't make it someplace else
because maybe we only get one chance
to walk off with a win, and this was it.

Season's End

He stares at the styrofoam steaming
the way his breath escapes, empties it
on the sidewalk, sweeps it down the block
with last night's garbage—hot dog wrappers,
peanut shells, a T-shirt, ticket stubs.
They've got a kid on the way and he's
worried his wife will have to give up
her job at the Stop n' Shop. He takes
a seat with the other janitors,
hardly speaks. All season, he didn't
watch a game, couldn't bring himself to
look at players younger than him, arms
gracing through the heavy air, a ball
snapped across the field the way a scar
stretches over an elbow. Crowds cheered
while he mopped bathrooms. He tells the guys
his brother-in-law might let him drive
a plow for extra cash this winter.
He pictures snow in headlights—halos
of mosquitoes around the outfield
lights, his summers playing ball, long days,
warm nights. But then there's winter streets—
slush clogs the gutters, every corner looks
as good a place as any to stop
the engine, get out, walk away, leave

everything that's leaving him behind.
He remembers those summers the way
you recall, falling asleep, the face
of a lover who left and hasn't
come back. He remembers those summers
every morning there's frost, as the fall
gives in and even the sunlight's frail.

Taking Flight

He leans against an empty oil drum to smoke
as traffic crawls beside the river. The day

drops behind the empty mills, its shadows
stretched across a picture of his kids.

The bell rings him out to another car
before he gets to finish his cigarette.

He rubs his hands on his Dickies, fingers
burning from the cold. He curses, hustles

car to car, checking oil and washing windows
for strangers who thank him but don't look up.

When he sleeps he sees his kids taking
flight, wings unfolding, eyes fixed on the hills

past the city limits; they never look down
at the growing pile of ash. He's always liked

the smell of gas, how it stings his nose, stays
in his clothes, soaks his skin. How easily he'd light—

sparks from a dragging tailpipe, a flicked cigarette—
how high the flare, how quickly he'd burn up.

Appleton & Pearl

Sunset, we work our way through town, drive
    down the alley where my father's garage still leans

between buildings turned over to ghosts
    and whispers slip through cracked glass.

I take it slow around the corner, stop
    to let a kid cross. He's already stepped

off the curb, ignores the winter muck, walks on.
    His eyes like faded coins stare back. Almost

dark, I take your hand. You've wanted me to explain
    anger: eyes sharpened, fierce, short words dropped.

We've passed over cobblestones worn smooth, past
    the famous diner, rundown, empty, under

the tired watch of fire-stained brick. Canals,
    churches, boardinghouses, all of it surprised you:

marble, granite, names and dates, ornate facades
    on vacant buildings, liquor stores and pawn shops,

a place that peddles postcards, snow globes, spools
    of thread they say was made in the mills.

Now, toes warming under the seat as darkness
    rushes these streets, can you hear it? The eyes

always tell. They say it better than poems, better
    than the moon hiding its face behind a cloud.

Dust

Before I'd ever read a poem
I traced my name in dust
wherever it settled, traced
it over and over—in pollen
on a windowsill, grime
on dad's workbench—letters
overlapping, tangled knots
of naming. Lost in the loop
of language, I'd imagine
myself walking the roads
I'd laid down, canyon walls
of dust looming above me.
In an Oregon classroom
it sprawled across the table
like the early pages of a poem.
Books with cracked spines
rested on cluttered shelves, walls
pasted over with faded flyers.
I'd shake off raindrops and take
my place. We grew to know
each other's imperfections
as our own, young poets
with sheaves of empty paper
we felt the need to fill. Later

I'd hold my poems close
to my body and emerge
into sinking sunlight.
Every shaft filtered the dust
that descends and settles
in every crevice of this life,
innumerable comets of grief
to be ciphered into new
existences, every line worked
into knowable shapes until
something like a soul stretches
across every turning day.

To the Guy Who Stole My Bike

I'm sorry if it sucked—it must have been a pain in the ass
to cut a chain wound tight as my eyes in sleep. Be careful:
once I went over the handlebars and took skin off both hands
and knees. Don't worry, I haven't ridden in a while—I take
the bus and read a book—so it's no big deal. A kid once stole
my hat and tossed it in a river. War stole mom's first love. Booze
took one grandfather, cancer another—cancer almost got
my brother too. (I'm two, it's Christmas, and we come home
from the hospital—he's spent weeks struggling to breathe
and getting surgery and radiation—to discover someone's broken
into the house and found we have nothing to steal so smashed
a few windows for fun.) Sometimes I imagine you ride it
every day like I did when I bought it. (It took me a summer
cleaning toilets to save up and then my folks pitched in
so I would have a bike at school.) I figure you sold it, hopefully
to help with tuition or books or to splurge on porterhouse steaks
and wine or whiskey, weed. Please don't let me know
you ditched it in the creek. I want you to enjoy it and never
think of me and what I've lost, what you could never take.

Each Pleasure

I used to work
with a guy

who'd stick
his pinky in the vise

and crank it
till sweat popped

from the pores
on his forehead.

When I asked him why
of course he said it felt

so goddamn good
when he stopped.

He'd smile despite
the spite, spit on the floor,

mutter fuck me
when he meant fuck you—

screw it all, it's
all of it shit—

but still
he'd buy a round—

bury me upside down
and kiss my ass,

stick with it long enough
enough's enough,

it's rough but not so bad,
it's not so bad

besides, two weeks
at the beach, each

bite of a wave, the breath
when a breaker breaks

against your belly, balls
like pebbles

shot through your gut,
got to admit

it's pretty good
and the rest of it

who gives a shit,
just give me this.

A hand cramped
around a handle

(hammer, blowtorch, broom)
beckons

the late-night longneck
bottle, becomes

a way to grip
the world, grasp

what you have
wherever you head

when the workday
ends, bends itself

around each pleasure
that passes your way.

My Father's Garage as Resting Place

Ivy crawls up cracks in concrete walls
I scraped and painted every summer. Built
in the forties and meant to hunker

against the worst New England can give,
its windows frame the river and its willows.
It's easy to see why my father bought it—

what better place for his big bones
and broad shoulders and hands like granite
to get run down by eleven-hour days?

The cops used to sit in the office, coffee
and donuts, smoking and shooting the shit:
hockey games and heart attacks, kids away

at school, the boobs on a beauty walking by.
Now they park at the edge of the lot, watch
for traffic running the red across the bridge.

The gas pumps are gone and the new owners
hung their sign above the double bays.
Next door the redbrick church is empty

almost every day, the ivy spreading
to its wrought iron fence. There's always
a steady parade of cars, always the river

passing, winter always on its way,
but weeping willows are the first to bear leaves
in spring and the last to let them fall.

The Truth Is

I'd like to begin with landscape, how clouds floated above hills
in the haze of morning's divinity: *I watch the sun setting*

on the Merrimack, orange blazing on the oily surface. Nothing stops
tears, thoughts of watching this river run past me the rest of my life.

But I've looked to the sky too many times, to snowcapped peaks
in distance, hoping for a sign, and too many times I've written lies:

fears and solitude, dejection on darkening days, midnight silenced by snow;
hints of immortality, dawning of love upon me in bright blue of spring.

The truth is:
our parents pass away on mornings tulips bloom. I fell in love

in October, leaves falling at our feet. Lowell's seen its share
of sunshine, despite what I often say. The truth is: storms

reminded my grandfather not of war, but how his dog smelled in rain. Not everyone
stands beside a dirty river and thinks of every second of his life being worn away.

TWO

Because This Life Is Brief

Cathedrals rise over cobblestone towns.
Because this life is brief we learn to write
    our names in granite. [There is elegy
because this life is brief.] We make stories

"Death is the Mother of beauty."

    from patterns we come across in the stars
but the dead don't see the stars or feel
    the rain, and if space is really expanding
infinitely, then this life grows shorter
    with every shudder of the skies above.
[Because this life is brief and winter sleeps
    in our bones], we stretch every summer day
past the slip of darkness, to the silence
    when even the crickets call it a night
[and the moon slides behind the empty mills
    as we wait, watching for stars to come down.]
Because even the stars will one day fail.
    A man who understands his life is brief
rides elevators all the way up to see
    the streets of his home like never before,
or maybe takes the stairs and stops at every
    floor to speak with every perfect stranger.
But if my father could write a poem from
    wherever the dead find themselves after
they die, I imagine he'd write a poem
    that says to stay outside and wait for rain,
to watch how every drop holds light, to hear
    the hiss when it kisses the summer street.

Shopping for Pants as Lesson in Language

Every year we went to Sears to buy my pants for school, I'd say a prayer
in the dressing room, beg whoever was up there to let them fit, fight

back tears when belly bulged over waistband, wait for Mom and Dad
to drag me to the rack at the back of the store, its tags labeled *husky*—

slacks for fat kids, stubby legs and no waist, chubby cheeks spreading the seat.
I've learned in language there are no absolutes, but then I knew nothing

of signifier and signified, of what comes unsaid when we speak, how to say
husky is to not say *tall, thin, regular*—I hated the word itself.

In the beginning was the Word and the Word was with God, but when he dies
he asks: *Why have you forsaken me?* In another account: *It's finished.*

It's said the most common word for a child to speak first is *no*—
before all the naming, before awareness of every numinous thing:

negation, ability to deny, language of oblivion.
Once, before I knew it could be true, I wrote *our parents pass away*

on mornings tulips bloom. Then one April, dumbstruck, I stood amid flowers
beside a grave. No graceful passing on, no sunlit room, no words

of goodbye—he dropped, fell to the floor when it broke, artery unable to hold
its blood, dead in hours, pile of emptied clothes beside an emptied bed.

The Memory Endeavors to
Bear Its Own Weight

A leaf falls into the shadow of a tree
by the side of a road. All the little things

we leave behind, past. Shadows
of leaves shaking in wind, shadow of a tree.

. . .

Hour after hour I stood there, shaking
hands, tried to listen. Flowers everywhere:

daisies, lilies. I can recall only stillness,
the stillness of his face, his hands folded.

. . .

Every drop of rain falls by itself
and still we speak of storms

as seasons meander and never come
into anything other than themselves.

. . .

A photographer, in his entire life,
hardly gets more than twenty minutes

on film—fractions of fractions of seconds
at a time. What falls between shots:

. . .

lost, the light between shadows
of untold leaves we see as a tree.

→ death / Elegy is a flush of
pain amidst life

Funeral with Cherry Blossoms Falling

I

April's softened
the soil—snowmelt,
weeks of rain. Now
the skies are empty
except for a blackbird
diving down, searching
for earthworms among
the green that spread
almost overnight
underfoot. Six feet
of dirt's deeper
than I'd imagined:
there's no getting out
again. Everyone's left
through the cemetery
gates and I'm waiting
with the guy in coveralls
who seems surprised
I've stayed. He keeps
his eyes turned down
to the gash he's made
in the grass, his own
shadow creeping
toward its edge. When it's time
he looks to me.
I nod and he drops
to a knee, flips
a switch that slowly
lowers the casket down.

2

The sun summits
another day and starts
to sink. The wind
whips scant branches,
lets loose a shower
of blossoms like
winter's final flurry.
Everything, it seems,
is falling, everything
following my father
down, the earth,
falling into itself.

3

Stare at water falling
over a cliff's edge
long enough,
everything else
seems to float up:
rocks hover, trees
break from roots, leave
the nourishing ground
below. It's only
illusion, only
the eyes playing
a trick on the mind,
but for a moment
you can feel it all—
the very earth itself—
ascending.

→ moments in life are
  frozen

Sonnet for the Guy Who Told Me
My Dad Was a Saint

Lowell

Saints don't come from dumps like this. They come
from towns untransected by train tracks or tainted
rivers passing rows of molting tenements,
from cities where every block's a work of art

and spires scrape clouds, every window stained
in prayer. Sacred steps don't tread these streets:
even the blessed must feel the weight of brick,
history's consumptive grating in the chest.

But today—in the shade of a willow, water
gracing over the dam, walls of a mill rising up
to meet a ceiling of sistine sky—a saint's

not an impossible thing, and the dust slipping
through sunlight's almost beatific, almost
beatific and almost beautiful.

Elegy with a Chance of Rain

There's an owl overhead, beneath
my feet acorns cracking, ground.
Fog hides stars, dims what light persists
up there. Darkness, the cold undoing

of winter coming. Tomorrow's six months
since he left us, even longer since
rain, a summer of utter sky, crows
wheeling in the endlessness.

I remember New Hampshire, his first
vacation since he was a kid. A week
of rain, day after gray day drumming
on the aluminum roof, the firewood

waterlogged. We sat by the lake, waited
for Whale Rock to go under, imagined
the socked-in mountains. He said it felt
like it was letting up. I said I was bored.

He swore it would stop soon. Next morning
I woke to silence above, yellow light, smell
of drying rain, puddles shrinking into
themselves, dandelions, tufts of grass

grown wild. Rain seemed suddenly absurd,
something I'd only heard about
in someone else's dream. The unblinking
sun seemed to promise it had been there

all along, would stay put. Like so much else
the weather always seems to steal in
under cover of dark and I'm never
quite sure what's memory and what dream.

An owl's overhead, and fog—tomorrow's
forecast calls for rain. Whatever's left
up there, let it come. Let another winter
smuggle in its stars behind these passing clouds.

[untitled]

Life passes at the speed of grief:

every morning another sun,

every night a different darkness.

November: Almost New Moon

All day the clouds shrouded Windy Hill
but seemed empty threats. Now the blacktop
glistens. I can't hear the rain, can't see
it dropping against white skies. The oaks

unravel for winter. I watch them
for hours, haven't caught a single
leaf falling. There's so much to be missed,
so much I'd give anything to have

back. At Saint Joseph's Cemetery
the ground's starting to freeze; it won't be
long before my father's name is lost
under a mantle of snow. The last

of the swallows have taken to flight,
and smoke begins to wisp from houses,
hovers over vacant lots. A world
away I shuffle through fallen leaves

as the rain lets up. Twilight's long gone
and clouds, dissolving, reveal the stars
spinning, indifferent as they always
are, staggering through so much darkness.

Song

I worry that I'm losing
my ear. Nothing sounds enough,
nothing's full. Everything limps
to the end and breaks. A poem
might as well be a species
account of snowy plovers,
a scientists' notes on sex
determination among
gators, a study of how
bats navigate the darkness
by ear. I've been reading all
of it—cookbooks, histories
of mapmakers, math—mining
every bibliography
for Rosetta stones to teach
the language I've lost. It's all
dull. Tuneless din, the same old
prayers we offer up before
the caskets of those we love
from the first, when everything
sounded, when every breath was
a note strung for the only
time. A bat finds its way by
listening for the echoes
of its own silent screams—how
tenuous the lines of song
that tether us to this world.

New Year's Eve

Not quite nine o'clock, new
year riding waves across
Atlantic darkness, dad
not gone nine months, the phone
rings again: we're about
to lose our grandfather
now. This year can't get gone
fast enough. And the next
when it breaks will leave us
with a shore we hardly
recognize, the way most
sea changes come—sudden,
complete, unrelenting.

→ Grief creates
a new reality

Poem with the Glimmer
of Ice in a Tree

Dogs crying out
across the river
seem to know
what we don't—
every moment
there's something
worth weeping for.
The wind shifts
snowdrifts, scours
the stippled ice
that hides the river
sneaking itself
out to sea. Cold
enough for tears,
gray seeps
into the eyes
of everyone
who passes by.
I hear the howls
of those abandoned
dogs, remember
all this year's taken
away. Behind me
a procession
of dull cars

waits for the light
to change. Even
the circling gulls
seem to falter, lost
in the leaden skies
while a willow's
bare branches glisten,
bent, ready to break
under such a weight.

Late March

All winter men with shovels
    cleared the little streets, tree-lined
        paths through snow and ice. Still

you never showed. The ground
    now turning soft with every
        lengthening day, the melting

and mud, the sun, this season
    offers rain to wash away
        the stain of earth from clothes,

from bones. Rise and show yourself.
    Cup your hands to hold it, rinse
        the slumber from your eyes. Rise

and look again at what begins
    to grow. See the roads you used
        to know. Find your way back home.

[handwritten annotation: — from the story? cemetery? from death?]

As If Souls Really Do Ascend

Winter's winding down
with another week
of rain—almost April
again, almost a year—
and it makes no sense:
an overheated car
on the other side
of the freeway, steam
like breath against
the steady drizzle.
Dad spent his days
under hoods of cars,
sweating into puddles
of grease. He taught me
the blowtorch is hottest
where it's blue. The same
brush that scrapes away
the melting metal
knocks off the caps
good as a hammer
but without dents
or cracks—solder them
to a new core, save
the customer some cash.
We'd clean the whole thing

in scalding water, paint it
black, put it back in
almost good as new.
But it's almost April
again, almost a year
my father's gone;
there'll be no saving
this car's radiator.
In the distance silent
hills send up steam,
every tree a candle
put out by the rain
as traffic crawls along,
another procession
working its way toward dark.

53

The Gravedigger to the Grieving Poet

Don't talk to me about your river of loss,
your uncut hair of graves. Don't read me your poems
for the dead. I've seen what happens to the dead

in poems: they rise as dust in a shaft of light,
as wind in trees, as dandelions cracking
the pavement of a potholed road in April.

I got news for you: a word is elegy
for no life worth living. No consolation
comes, remember, unless you walk out those gates

and get on with living, flip the page, forget.
You lay them to rest. I spend my every day
with them. I figure you'll put me in a poem

but I sure wish you wouldn't. It's got nothing
to do with you, what I do. Plenty of days
I dig holes in the rain, but they don't make me

metaphor. I also cut the summer grass
and nap in the chapel. I shovel walkways
all winter and smoke behind the tallest stone.

I lock up the gates at night. Mornings I pass
from name to name and gather up the dying
flowers that nobody thinks to come back for.

Spring Comes to Lowell

Like the moon
lifting itself shadow
by shadow over
weary cities, winter
loosens its hold, leaves
potholes, rubbish
crusted to mounds of soot-
streaked snow and slush.
At Flaggie's Field
kids unwind winter
legs around the bases
as the sun sets, still
too soon for everyone
to get a chance to hit.
A lonely woman walks
along the swollen river
where a cottonwood's
scattering its seeds
in search of fertile
soil. There's no bird-
song on the breeze
but on the other bank
a freight train whistles
something of arrival.
Slowly, a living

earth emerges
through its shell—
it falters, tentative,
the way we begin
to accept the dead
aren't coming back.

Portrait of My Father as a Mountain

Up here your every breath becomes part of the clouds. Streaks
of fog descend into valleys like tranquil rivers, dawn-gray.

When the sun shines the valleys are like valleys, stretch away
as shadows of trees, spaces between, embrace rocky streambeds.

Black spruce and balsam fir drip beads like sweat from the brow
of a climber scrambling cairn to cairn through the summit scrub.

You bow your head against a quick wind. It rips around you, flips
your hood, brings tears. It's clouds and valleys below, so much life

spread out before you, spinning out to every point, reeling.
It makes you feel weightless, timeless grinding, granite falling

away, sloping out from under you. You can't go any higher
so you add a rock to a cairn, make the peak just that much taller.

So much passes, has already passed, without our seeing.
To really see the mountain, you'd have to walk away, look back

from time to time as it gathers itself up, fades against the dusk.
Up here the mountain's only the ground beneath your feet.

Lines from Wherever My Father Finds Himself

Make a mix and listen to songs I made up words to,

every *la la la* let loose with gusto, bluster, love.

Keep my number in your phone, frame the photo of us

reading in the rocking chair, hang my clothes in the back

of your closet. Before drinking beer, sprinkle a pinch

of salt, watch the carbonation rising and rising

and recognize me in the glass behind the bar while

outside rain keeps falling. Raise a toast and make a joke,

laugh with whoever stands beside you. Dance with strangers.

Talk to me where you happen to be—stuck in traffic,

grilling steaks and baseball on the radio, staring

at silent ceilings in the dark—speak my name and know

by its syllables that you are, by your breath forming

around each sound. There is no holy ground so don't stop

by the gravesite searching for me. I'm not there. But look:

this time of year cherry blossom buds come back, and grass

outgrowing winter gives the dandelions space to

make a home, no matter how fleeting, how brief. A path

leads past the chapel and out the gate—follow it back

to the waiting world, world I want to be remembered

in, another song you'll never get out of your head.

THREE

North of Stinson Beach

A quartet of pelicans like a measure of music in flight,
every wave crashing keeps the impossible rhythm:

erosion and decay under blue sky. Fog creeps closer
to the coast, reminds me something's always about to happen,

every moment becoming a past we water down
with each retelling, every place another home

we can't return to. Times like now, I don't know why
I bother writing any of it down—there is no line

between sea and sky, no telling when flow turns to ebb.
Everything passes imperceptibly enough to be missed,

unspeakably missed, the way our every breath becomes
the air itself. Every winter the sand's stripped away

by surging storms, brought back bit by bit, the sculpted rocks
unrecognizable month to month. And yet, every year

the snowy plovers return, their song never drowned out
by the surf, this language of give and take, language of grief.

Tending the Fire

There are stars so far away
      their light has yet to reach us
            and when it finally shines

on us, the stars themselves
      will have already fizzled out.
            The things of this world

never go away—matter's
      neither created nor destroyed.
            A log in the fireplace, hushed

voices in the night, you can see
      the universe at work: a knot pops,
            becomes smoke, heat, light, ash.

It's said that the dead live on
      in the memories of the living.
            That's also where they're always

leaving. Sparks bursting bear little
      likeness to the smoldering
            piles of morning's first light.

Ceiling: Unlimited

What to do
when nothing
crawls across
an empty sky?
I can't recall
the smell of rain
stippling asphalt
or snow about
to make its slow
accumulation.
A passing cloud
I tell myself
will revise this
shadowed ground.
Days like this
the blue gives a hint
of endlessness
I disbelieve,
having seen
sparrows fly
at windowpanes.
Who wouldn't
long to be
the carpenter,
the typist,

the drummer:
restless hands
tapping the steady
irregular
rhythms of rain?
I'd be wrong
to believe this wind
washing over me
is a blessing.
But I'd be lying
if I wrote
on days like this
I don't imagine
every oak's branches
lift in prayer
for this cracked
and fractured earth.

Prayer

Give me the moment when light fails,
when mountain peaks become one
starless sky swallowing a silver moon.

Give me all the moments between
dream and waking, stories of days
and night unfolding one silence

in near dark, where flying seems likelier
than my spoken name. Let me hear
myself unnamed, as near to dying

as toes grinding sand, high tide come
in, storm clouds slipping together
and breaking apart. Let me swim

into morning, engulfed by sea and sky;
let me test the waters, taste the unseen
salt, tell others, warn them of the cold.

I have held my breath for thunder
to call, missed the scent of one I almost
loved, fallen through a winter pond. Let me

have it, give me darkness of many nights,
shadow; grant me always another day.

Tonight I Walked in the Shadow of a Tree

The darkness chattered with crickets, leaves,
a feral cat in the bushes. Tonight
I walked behind my rising breath. I was
lonely and it was dark. An owl sounded

overhead and I was struck by winter
stars, a scrim of cloud, a waning moon—
it loomed between branches, lay its light
lightly on the ground beneath my feet,

luminescence amid limbs of dim shade.
The latticework of every day and night
is stunning in its constancy. Lately
it's the little things I find surprising,

tonight: the moon and its borrowed light
like looking one morning in the mirror
and seeing something of your father's eyes
you thought you'd never see again.

Even a Beach in Winter

FOR TREGONY

Most nights I lie awake with her
breathing, wait for it to lead me

away from the world. I listen
and tell myself I'm not alone,

that even a beach in winter
has the chatter of sanderlings

feeding on every ebbing wave.
Today I walked up Waddell Creek

and came across an abandoned
fire, the scent of sage blowing

through redwoods, every breath of smoke
a sentence I could almost grasp

the meaning of. I asked myself
why love's most whole when it resides

in silences—if she'd been there
she'd have walked ahead and waited

without a word, held her hand
at just the height for mine to find

and not let go of. The fire
embering, I made my way

back to the beach, the ocean still
trying to lull the birds to sleep.

After Rain

The wind comes warm as breath
and stirs me like laundry
on a line. Then it's gone. Life
weaves itself together
from next to nothing;
it's all these moments
I want, to take them in
before they're taken away.
A patch of blue breaches clouds
the way green comes to winter
and the black of a raven's
something I can hardly stand
the beauty of: unshadowed
or itself a shadow
untethered from things. It coasts
across the opening sky
on motionless wings
as if it too notices
a ray of light threading
its way into the world.

Working the Garden

FOR KATE

Today I've been remembering
    summer squash; strawberries
        ripening; cucumber vines

wound through chicken wire
    the way life and its absence are
        threaded between lines of a poem;

apples proving gravity's
    gentle tug, the constant pull
        of an underworld shrouded

in the aroma of loam, limbs
    lifting back into place, relieved
        of their cumbersome load;

and you, mending a hole
    in the fence, the guilty bear
        not even hiding. She peered

over tall grass, lifted her chin
    as if laughing, amused
        you'd be fixing what she'll wreck

again, bemused you haven't
    given up, haven't let yourself
        believe in wastes of time.

I watched you patch it together
        lovingly, line by wire line
            like a story told and retold

until only a character's name
        stays the same. The hardest part's
            knowing no animal, not one

of us, will ever learn to be
        content with the fruit
            shaken loose from the branches

that stretch beyond a fence.
        Later we spoke in voices hushed
            by the summer night until all

that remained was wind
        in Douglas-firs, the river's
            not-so-distant roar: sounds

we learn to call silence,
        a word I still can't bring
            myself to believe in.

Poem with Snowy Plovers

April's only days
away. The wind strokes
sandstone cliffs, the cove
empty except for
snowy plovers.
A grain of sand
brings tears. An ocean
is beautiful
in its cruelty—last
week, currents swept
someone out to sea—
so I'm watching
for rogue waves, don't
notice the puddle
that soaks my shoe.
I'm able to laugh
at almost all of it.
Squinting against
the sun as it breaks
through, I watch wind-
whipped waves, a host
of birds taking flight.

Under a Summer Sky

FOR CHRIS

We sit around a fire and trace
      constellations, trying to translate
the stories our fathers told. Wind

      sighs in a bottle, and you wrap
a blanket around your son, who asks
      how many shooting stars can there be

in a night. You answer for all of us
      it depends on how dark the night gets.
The fire snaps a spray of sparks

      that peters out in the emptiness
above. A moth circles, and I know
      the first wish was made not on stars

but on spaces between: the unfillable
      dark that lets us recognize
a trickle of light from so far away.

At a Horseshoe Bend in the Rogue

A salmon leaps up, wholly out,
floats a half-foot off the surface,

every drop on every silver scale
a different shade of shining sun.

Quick as it rose, it goes back down
through currents, upstream. It leaves

behind spreading rings, waves, a tide
of light that doesn't reach the riverbank.

It's easy to imagine a fish would
want to breathe the warm of sunsets,

dream of leaving its water, risk
the weightless pleasures above,

easy to pretend its eye, before
it drops from sight, holds mine, a moment

of universal speech, shared struggle
against dark waters, the quiet of night.

A Constant Reminder

FOR SIS AND TED

A bowl friends sent
as a wedding gift
scatters sunshine
across the floor,
the glassblower's
every imperfection
making the light
our own. We piece
a life together
from what we're given,
remake ourselves
by what we give.
Walk in the woods
and you'll learn
redwoods begin
when one gives itself back
to earth, seedlings sprouting
in a ring around it;
as they grow, a circle
holds an emptiness
of light, imparts
an immortality
even as the space

remains a constant
reminder of absence.
We must come to love
the permanence of all
this impermanence:
today I learned
that owls, instead
of building their own,
use the abandoned
nests of other birds
the way the moon
traces the sun's path
across a limitless sky.

Life After Life

It is a certain satisfaction to overlook a cemetery.
WILLIAM CARLOS WILLIAMS

It's easy to be impressed with such order: an orchard
seen at seventy miles an hour. Row after row

of paths between trees, precise, not a limb out of place.
Straight lines stretched across and back toward distant hills

of dust, each tree a point on six lines—geometric
certainties against the chance of drought or early frost.

. . .

It's easy to be impressed with a mile of mills, hard lines
of brick on brick six stories high, sharp corners, stern

clock towers and smokestacks rising to preside
over rows of identical tenements. Canals carved

in granite to straighten the river's path, intricate
system of locks and gates. Beyond the city

limits, acres and acres of workers at rest
and plotted as flat and straight as rolling hills allow:

polished stones, names and dates impeccably inscribed. Life
after life filed away beneath trim green fields.

. . .

It's not impossible to imagine an orchard
from the road as a cemetery: the dead, weary

of rest, risen through fertile ground and burst
into flame, each leaf a tongue of fire defying design.

. . .

Imagine the planter's pleasure each night: lines guided
by design, each seed in its row, certainty sown.

. . .

It's a different satisfaction to imagine
roadside flowers climbing a wire fence, working

their way across a field, overrunning row
after unswerving row, a blaze of wildflower

spreading unchecked—nature breaking into itself, life
after life, unruly impossible life overcoming the certain.

Where I Come From the Snow's Beginning To Stick

December's heavy in the clouds. As kids we'd wait
in the gathering dark, faces pressed to windows, kindle
faith that this would be more than just an early flurry.

When the snow starts to pick up, it's hard to tell
falling flakes from water rushing over the falls.
Cemeteries diminish, row after row like wrinkled clouds

seen from above. Each stone's a wave on a tranquil sea.
The mills are almost pretty, edges softened by drifts
drooping from rooftops. Brick-on-brick's almost

warm, almost looks like embers in ash. Riverfront
trees come back to life, fill with light from passing traffic.
Fathers leave work early, pull on extra flannel and heavy

gloves, shovel driveways, keep ahead of the forecast.
Kids watch from windows, trace their names in frost,
wrap themselves in blankets, wait for dads who congregate

on slippery sidewalks, curse the cold, watch it falling faster
and faster through the beam of a streetlight. Their breath,
as they talk, rises as if from a fire they warm their hands by.

Like a Chance to Begin Again

Merrimack frozen over, gulls circling
from the landfill seem lost, reeling across

what flowed only days ago. The old men
huddled beside the boathouse tell tales

they've told, overworked stories of girls
who warmed the longest nights even more

farfetched when muffled by parkas and scarves.
In the wind they walk like birds, shoulders

hunkered in case of black ice, as the shell
of snow capping a factory bulges

like winter about to molt and give us
some wickeder form of itself—

it's only a sliver of afternoon moon
cresting into sight the way my face

in the window almost glowed as I flew
to this place I haven't called home in years.

Something of Home

Late winter, thick water slashes over the dam, granite roaring

under its force, punished only for being there, for settling

in ancient mud. The city festers in its sleep. No boats. Canals

that don't move. This bridge above Pawtucket Falls, one a mile down

and between them it's red brick, plywood windows reflecting nothing.

When you're young, cities seem magnificent no matter what. Wide-eyed

you look up to all the buildings crowned with wreaths of ice, speak fondly

all the streets, mouth full with knowing *This is home.*

It's later leaving comes to you. You search for where the water's still

unmuddied, where the moon floats between branches reaching up and up.

And yet you leave and never leave. You stand beneath a lucent breath

of clouds that wax and wane and see the lights of Lowell rise and fall

on every wave. The river cuts deeper with every passing night.

ACKNOWLEDGMENTS

I AM GRATEFUL to the editors of the following publications in which some of these poems first appeared, sometimes in slightly different form.

Atticus Review: 'Lowell National Historic Park'; *Bellingham Review:* 'Because This Life Is Brief,' 'Like a Chance to Begin Again'; *Blueline:* 'Ceiling: Unlimited,' 'Portrait of My Father as a Mountain'; *Borderlands: Texas Poetry Review:* 'Where I Come From the Snow's Beginning to Stick'; *Boulevard:* 'At a Horseshoe Bend in the Rogue,' '[untitled]'; *Boxcar Poetry Review:* 'Funeral with Cherry Blossoms Falling'; *Breakwater Review:* 'The Memory Endeavors to Bear Its Own Weight'; *The Common* Online: 'After Rain,' 'Poem with Snowy Plovers'; *Cider Press Review:* 'Tending the Fire,' 'Working the Garden'; *Cossack Review:* 'Under a Summer Sky'; *Crab Orchard Review:* 'Elegy with a Chance of Rain,' 'Mill Town: Variations,' 'November: Almost New Moon,' 'Sonnet for the Guy Who Told Me My Dad Was a Saint'; *District:* 'Tonight I Walked in the Shadow of a Tree'; *The Fourth River:* 'The Truth Is'; *Heron Tree:* 'Late March'; *Hobble Creek Review:* 'The Canal,' 'Dust'; *Iron Horse Literary Review:* 'Song'; *Lake Effect:* 'Poem with the Glimmer of Ice in a Tree,' 'Spring Comes to Lowell'; *Mid-American Review:* 'The Gravedigger to the Grieving Poet'; *Moon City Review:* 'Each Pleasure'; *The Normal School:* 'Something of Home'; *North American Review:* 'Shopping for Pants as Lesson in Language'; *Poet Lore:* 'After a Student Prefaces Her Question about a Poem,' 'As If Souls Really Do Ascend,' 'City Champs Celebrate Unlikely Win in Back of Coach's Pickup'; *Potomac Review:* 'Life After Life'; *Prime Number:* 'My Father's Garage as Resting Place,' 'Morning Mass,' 'Taking Flight'; *Red Rock Review:* 'Poem for My Brother'; *Salamander:*

'Lines from Wherever My Father Finds Himself,' 'New Year's Eve';
Silk Road: 'Season's End'; *Smartish Pace:* 'North of Stinson Beach';
Sugar House Review: 'Nor'easter'; *Two Weeks: A Digital Anthology of Contemporary Poetry:* 'To the Guy Who Stole My Bike'; and *Valparaiso Poetry Review:* 'A Constant Reminder.'

I am grateful for opportunities to attend Amherst College, the Creative Writing Program at the University of Oregon, and the Bread Loaf Writers' Conference, and to all my teachers, including Constance Congdon, Garrett Hongo, Glyn Maxwell, Joseph Millar, William H. Pritchard, Tom Sleigh, Kim Townsend, Pimone Triplett, and especially Dorianne Laux. For their own work, for insightful readings of these poems, and for friendship, I am grateful to William Archila, Lory Bedikian, Miriam Gershow, Patrick Oh, and especially Kate Westhaver. I am deeply grateful to Arthur Smith for believing in these poems and to Chad Prevost, Terrence Chouinard, and C&R Press for bringing this book into being.

Many thanks to Theodore and Francis Geballe for their enthusiasm, to Donald and Susan Pogue for their support, and to Saul H. Benjamin for passing along a box of poetry when I needed it most. Endless thanks to my brother Scott, whose imagination has always inspired me, and to my mother Karen, whose love has always been a home. Special thanks to Jason Vermillion, whose friendship makes me a better version of myself. And most of all to Tregony, who day after day does more for me than I deserve: my deepest thanks and ever my love.

BRIAN SIMONEAU grew up in Lowell, Massachusetts, and graduated from Amherst College and the University of Oregon. His poems have appeared in *Boulevard, Crab Orchard Review, The Georgia Review, Mid-American Review,* and other journals. He lives in Connecticut with his wife and two daughters.

CPSIA information can be obtained at www.ICGtesting.com
Printed in the USA
BVOW04s0450251114

376606BV00001B/6/P